UNF#CK YOUR
BUSINESS
WORKBOOK

USING MATH AND BRAIN SCIENCE
TO RUN A SUCCESSFUL BUSINESS

JOE BIEL + DR. FAITH G. HARPER

Microcosm Publishing
Portland, OR | Cleveland, OH

UNFUCK YOUR BUSINESS WORKBOOK

Using Math and Brain Science to Run a Successful Business

© Joe Biel and Faith Harper, 2024

ISBN 9781621064695
This is Microcosm #617
First published March 2024
This edition © Microcosm Publishing, 2024

For a catalog, write or visit:
Microcosm Publishing
2752 N Williams Ave.
Portland, OR 97227
www.Microcosm.Pub/Business

To join the ranks of high-class stores that feature Microcosm titles, talk to your rep: In the U.S. **COMO** (Atlantic), **ABRAHAM** (Midwest), **BOB BARNETT** (Texas, Oklahoma, Arkansas, Louisiana), **IMPRINT** (Pacific), **TURNAROUND** (UK), **UTP/MANDA** (Canada), **NEWSOUTH** (Australia/New Zealand), **OBSERVATOIRE** (Africa, Middle East, Europe), **Yvonne Chau** (Southeast Asia), **HARPERCOLLINS** (India), **EVEREST/B.K. Agency** (China), **TIM BURLAND** (Japan/Korea), and **FAIRE** and **EMERALD** in the gift trade.

Did you know that you can buy our books directly from us at sliding scale rates? Support a small, independent publisher and pay less than Amazon's price at **www.Microcosm.Pub**.

This is a companion title to the 2023 book *Unfuck Your Business* by the same authors.

Global labor conditions are bad, and our roots in industrial Cleveland in the '70s and '80s made us appreciate the need to treat workers right. Therefore, our books are MADE IN THE USA.

MICROCOSM · PUBLISHING

Microcosm Publishing is Portland's most diversified publishing house and distributor, with a focus on the colorful, authentic, and empowering. Our books and zines have put your power in your hands since 1996, equipping readers to make positive changes in their lives and in the world around them. Microcosm emphasizes skill-building, showing hidden histories, and fostering creativity through challenging conventional publishing wisdom with books and bookettes about DIY skills, food, bicycling, gender, self-care, and social justice. What was once a distro and record label started by Joe Biel in a drafty bedroom was determined to be *Publishers Weekly*'s fastest-growing publisher of 2022 and #3 in 2023, and is now among the oldest independent publishing houses in Portland, OR, and Cleveland, OH. We are a politically moderate, centrist publisher in a world that has inched to the right for the past 80 years.

CONTENTS

STAGNATING LEADERS

Power comes from authority

Privatizes information

Discourages team from developing ideas

Dictates solutions to problems

Minimizes time & resources for problem solving

Believes in strict roles & responsibilities

Responds reactively to problems

Reviews staff performance once per year

EFFECTIVE LEADERS

Power comes from collaboration

Shares information

Encourages suggestions and ideas

Collectivizes solutions to problems

Allocates time and resources to prevent problems

Roles and responsibilities are fluid and evolve

Resolves root causes of problems

Provides immediate and ongoing feedback and personalized coaching

INTRODUCTION

*T*wo different people don't enter the world of entrepreneurship for the same reasons. In fact, that's a major reason for the vast diversity of small businesses and their respective strengths. I never intended to go into business, but I found it to be the least compromising way to make a living after a series of jobs where bosses didn't actually want me to make their systems more efficient or better serve the intended goals.

The way that it happened is rather funny. As a scheme to pay reduced car insurance rates, I attended business classes at my local community college for two quarters. During the first quarter, I was told that business plans have zero foundation in reality, facts, or citations. They are literally made-up, pie-in-the-sky dreams about what you would like to happen. Then you use these claims to ask people to give you money on the "strength" of the plan.

During my second quarter I was told that there is no mathematical formula to evaluate, judge, or review to know if your advertising spend was effective. At this point, I realized that since the entire world of business was laid on a foundation of bald-faced lies, these classes were not worth the insurance discount, and I dropped out. I believed that business should instead be a product of critical thinking, intensive analytical review, and thinking bigger. And 28 years later, I know how true this is.

On a walk the other day, it suddenly came to me: a functional business is the intersection between the four variables of supply, demand, scale, and access. If there's enough demand and not too much supply, you can produce at scale at a cost acceptable to consumers. If you have access to the resources and materials that you need, the business will succeed. Sure, you could complicate this by managing the company poorly or through being a tyrant to your staff, but in general, the principles are sound. I'm not sure why this just dawned on me in my 28th year running a publishing company, other than that I tend to avoid these "it's really this simple" proclamations. For once, though, I do believe that business is as simple as these four intersecting (and ever-moving) variables.

The sandwich shop on the corner has to face the same rules of economics as the international car maker, as does the food exporter, as does the real estate broker, as does the landlord or beverage distributor. Of course, factors can change and majorly complicate this. The cost of shipping containers can skyrocket, as we saw in 2021. The availability of labor may dry up as people realize that they don't actually *want* to sling coffee or pump gas or work in a slaughterhouse. As supply chains constrict, it may become much harder to get microchips, thus driving up the price of cars. You can't mine coltan in Nebraska; it generally has to come from Africa. The cost of eggs and cups may go up without the associated willingness of the consumer to pay these additional costs. The costs of paper and steel can rise out of control, and the government may ration them. If too many of these factors shift, a functional business may become a dysfunctional one, so it's important to review your budgets monthly, with a deeper review annually.

We'll revisit those items later, so let's not worry about them right now. Instead, let's focus on the six skills that you have to develop in business:

- Learning new things every day
- Eternally being an optimist
- Disregarding all bad news
- Doing what everyone tells you is impossible
- Keeping a sense of humor
- Recognizing good ideas before they are obvious in hindsight

Most good ideas are obvious, but only in hindsight. Because, well, you've just watched them work and create appealing and compelling value propositions. So the trick of the business owner is to identify good ideas at a time when everyone says, "If that would work, someone would be doing it already!" or "Kozmo already tried delivering random goods in 1999 and went out of business! Why would you succeed?" And then, 15 years later, there's dozens of specialty delivery businesses again for every imaginable product.

We're excitedly getting ahead of ourselves again. If you have an idea that you'd be excited to hop out of bed to work on on your own time on the weekends, with the understanding that it may only appeal to a few dozen people, but *you believe in it*—I think that you will likely succeed. If you would do it anyway, even if every adult in your life told you that it was a terrible idea, then you may have enough gusto in you to show the world how they underestimated you.

This workbook is a supplemental companion to *Unfuck Your Business*. Dr. Faith handles the emotional aspects of business, from imposter syndrome to the weight of family of origin expectations, while Joe tackles the nuts and bolts of how to do each thing, how to know if you are successful, and how to get to the next stage of your growth. This workbook can be used as a standalone, and it's fine to simply open to any page and complete the exercises. However, you may find it most valuable if you work through the exercises in order while reading the accompanying book.

This workbook is for anyone starting a new business or growing or purchasing an existing business. While most business books are focused on things like liability, taxes, control, legal structure, and industries with the most potential—all of which are too singular yet too broad to tackle in a book like this—we focus more on the practical and emotional aspects of running a business at any size and scale. The tools here are remarkably unchanged by the passage of time. So we'll spend as much time on imposter syndrome and not working out your childhood issues publicly as we will on interpreting your annual data and revising projections based on what you are seeing. Most importantly, if you want to improve your leadership skills, planning strategy, systems thinking, self-confidence, and financial literacy, this is likely the workbook for you!

You shouldn't feel the least bit underprepared for business because you don't know these things already. You don't know them because you didn't learn them. And you didn't learn them because in school you learned that mitochondria is the powerhouse of the cell, not how to balance a budget. We won't get into our beef with school systems here, because that is really a whole other book. Suffice to say, no one learns this stuff the way we are supposed to learn it. So you are being really smart and proactive by finding the information you need on your own. And Faith kindly requests that if you run into Mrs. Meisenheimer out in the wild anywhere, please let her know that Faith is doing just fine running a thriving business despite sucking at cursive writing and never holding her scissors properly.

Now, if you're still with us, let's get started.

Part One:

Make a Plan

*T*o begin a new business or grow or purchase an existing business, most owners are tasked with writing a "business plan." As we discussed, these are well-formatted lies compiled with falsified statistics and are primarily used to promote a rosy picture and to beg for money. That's fine, no shade, and I absolutely understand why people do this. But, you've got to ask yourself where you want to go before you decide how to get there. I'd be much more interested in knowing whether my concept would actually work. This is called "product market fit" (PMF) in business. I'm experienced enough now after 28 years that I can do these calculations in my head, but for most business owners in their first 10 years, the goal should instead be to mitigate possible causes of failure.

If a business has poor PMF, you can pump limitless amounts of money and time into marketing and promotion and it simply won't move the needle. No matter how many people you reach, your product doesn't fit the market. Sometimes the cost of acquiring customers (CAC) is simply too great and you cannot afford to exist. Running an organization with good PMF is like playing a video game on easy mode:

- It just feels like excited people come to you with their wallets open.
- People constantly send you resumes and ask if you're hiring, unsolicited.
- You don't need to think too much about marketing or how to reach people because it seems to happen on its own.

If you aren't seeing these things, you want to adjust your product until you do. And while we're on the subject of failure, here's something to keep in mind: The fact that someone else failed at doing the same thing doesn't mean that you will fail too. It means that you have to solve the problems that they were unable to. I once met someone who insisted that she was starting a prepared-meals delivery company that would simultaneously be cheaper than HelloFresh and pay a living wage. I asked her where she would obtain a budget surplus while reducing her income. Her best answer was "reducing corporate greed." But the reality is that most startup businesses like these are funded by venture capital, not actual sales of products and services.

So in this first part of the workbook, we'll focus on the basics of business success: determining whether your business is viable, refining your mission and brand, and getting out of your own way.

THE VALUE CHAIN

Business is about aligning the value chain and incentives at every stage. This means looking at the steps of every decision and outcome from beginning to end, and evaluating how they create value for everyone involved. For example, when Joe's company, Microcosm Publishing, publishes a book, everyone benefits up and down the value chain: the printer, the retailers, the author, the readers, and the publisher. When revenues exceed expenses, our staff receives profit sharing. This means that when the value chain is aligned, nobody is at odds with each other. We have the same goals and, through working together to accomplish them, we all win. If your value chain is out of alignment, you will notice, even if no one says anything.

VRRR

DO I HAVE WHAT IT TAKES?

*T*he hip-hop artist Jay-Z, who has sold over 100 million albums and is worth $2.5 billion, offers in his book, *Decoded*, business advice he learned as a street drug dealer that also applies to most businesses. The pop quiz below is based partly on his rules for business success. For each of these questions, score yourself on a scale of 1–5, where 1 is "not good at all" and 5 is "extremely good."

1. How good are you at doing quick math in your head? ○*1* | ○*2* | ○*3* | ○*4* | ○*5*

2. How good are you at judging character? ○*1* | ○*2* | ○*3* | ○*4* | ○*5*

3. How are your critical thinking skills? ○*1* | ○*2* | ○*3* | ○*4* | ○*5*

4. How is your attention to detail? ○*1* | ○*2* | ○*3* | ○*4* | ○*5*

5. How is your work ethic? ○*1* | ○*2* | ○*3* | ○*4* | ○*5*

6. How good are you at making quick decisions? ○*1* | ○*2* | ○*3* | ○*4* | ○*5*

Add up your total. _____ It will often surprise you how useful these skills are in the field. Now use the following questions to reflect on your results.

How do you feel about the results?

_____

_____

How can you work on improving your responses in your weakest areas?

_____

_____

How can you develop each of these skills for your profession?

_____

_____

What tasks are your skills and strengths best suited for?

_____

_____

What tasks should you really enlist others to do?

_____

_____

Who is someone you trust and respect who you can process unfolding details with?

_____

_____

That's not the only list of skills to consider though. Remember the six basic skills that you need to be an unshakeable operator, which we went over in the introduction? This exercise will help you further understand and develop these skills in yourself.

What new things do or can you focus on learning every day to grow your business acumen?

_____

_____

What are some ways that you are an eternal optimist? How can you lean further into rational self-belief?

_____

_____

How can you practice critical thinking skills to understand how best to react to bad news?

_____

_____

In what situations are you motivated to do what everyone tells you is impossible? How do you maintain perspective at these times?

_____

_____

What helps you to keep a sense of humor?

_____

_____

How can you improve your ability to distinguish between good and bad ideas in the moment, without the benefit of hindsight?

_____

_____

Next, we are going to look deeper at fundamentals. These are items that are usually ignored in business, or where ego gets in the way of results. When explaining their actions, people tend to focus on the context of the specific situation. But we're going to reframe this thinking by focusing instead on agency; because the situation doesn't dictate your actions—your decisions dictate your actions. For each prompt below, try to give an honest answer, keeping in mind that you are only sharing it with yourself.

Business owners tend to simultaneously attempt to control *everything* while failing to recognize what lands within their own agency to fix. Reflect on the following graphic and think about a specific problem that you are having, related to business or in your larger life.

What is bothering me?

What part of it is under my control?

What parts can I let go of?

What action can I take?

Half of business is exercising agency over what you can control and understanding what is happening in the context around you. Answer the following questions while thinking about your business in the broadest sense possible:

What do I need to know?

_____

_____

What do I need to accept?

_____

_____

What do I need to try?

_____

_____

What do I need to grieve?

_____

_____

What do I need to celebrate?

_____

_____

How should I react to various circumstances?

_____

_____

Now answer those same questions about a specific instance or problem:

What do I need to know?

_____

_____

What do I need to accept?

_____

_____

What do I need to try?

_____

_____

What do I need to grieve?

_____

_____

What do I need to celebrate?

_____

_____

How should I react to various circumstances?

_____

_____

HOW DO I KNOW IF MY BUSINESS WILL WORK?

*I*n the companion book to this workbook, I created a simple litmus test for success. My cousin, a certified public accountant of 30 years, gave me some of the best advice regarding formulas. She said, "It doesn't matter if your formula is 'correct,' it matters that you use it *consistently*." To test whether what you are doing will work, consider this equation:

(Demand / Supply) x Credibility x Access = *How Successful You Will Be*

Supply is how many other organizations are already offering your service or a similar one.

Demand is how popular your product or service is.

Credibility is the trustworthiness and reliability that you need to make a sale.

Access is your ability to reach the people that would benefit from what you do.

If you cannot sell something, it always comes down to a failure in one or more of these things: too much competing supply, not enough demand, not enough credibility, or insufficient access.

If you are less trained in experimental mathematics, you may be looking for simple numbers to plug in there that will tell you the answer. But success is variable, right? So what matters is that more supply is a larger number, more demand is a larger number, more credibility is a larger number, and more access is a larger number. This way, by honestly applying the same criteria, you can evaluate various ideas against each other. Let's give it a try.

Supply: What are some organizations that are already offering your product/service or a similar one in the same market? Your supply is how much overlap you have with these competitors. (E.g., there are three barber shops within one mile.)

_____

_____

_____

_____

Demand: What are some key indicators of the consumer demand for your product/service? (E.g., everyone in your neighborhood gets their hair cut every week, influencers can't stop talking about the kinds of haircuts you offer.)

_____

_____

_____

_____

Credibility: What makes you seem trustworthy within your market/field? How can you increase your level of credibility? (E.g., you've been giving this haircut for years and practically invented it.)

_____

_____

_____

_____

Access: What is your current level of access to your target market/audience? How can you improve access? (E.g., you hang out at the same places as all of the haircut fanatics.)

_____

_____

_____

_____

What's working in your equation? What isn't working?

_____

_____

Next we're going to look at changing variables in your market. I managed a successful Italian restaurant until a chain competitor moved in on the same block. Suddenly, our sales were cut in half. Sometimes factors change in your business that force you to change in order to remain viable. Let's take a look at some of these factors using the following graph exercise:

For supply, demand, price, and material availability, mark a dot where your product lands, then draw a line to the center and create a box. If the majority of your box is in the shaded area, your business is viable.

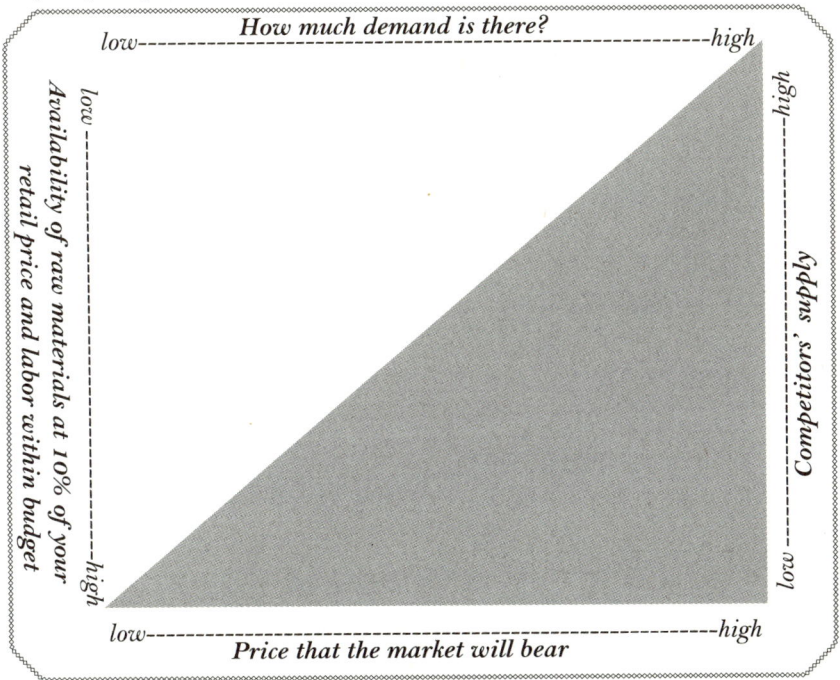

No matter what measurement system you use, the important thing is that you use it consistently and that it works *for your purposes*. So much of business is trying to convince someone else of something, so you need to stop and focus on how to make concepts simple so that you can work through them.

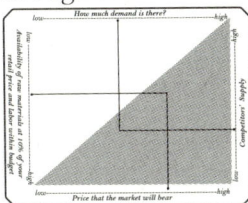

Viable

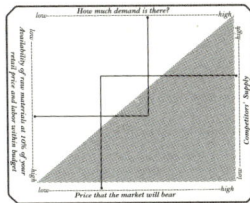

Difficult to make viable

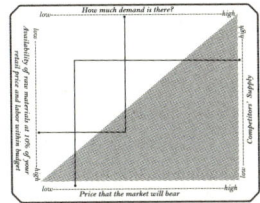

Not viable

STAYING GROUNDED IN THE BASICS

Next, we will focus on incremental growth and functional systems with the idea that you are building something to last. This requires some reflection on the fundamentals of why you're in the business, what problem you're solving, and how you're approaching it. You won't know the answers to all of these questions perfectly right now, but answer them as best you can and revisit them every six months or so.

Why are you passionate about and interested in this business?

_____

_____

On the most basic level, what problem are you solving?

_____

_____

Why are you qualified to solve it?

_____

_____

What is your most basic service? How does it solve this problem?

_____

_____

How are competitors solving this problem?

_____

_____

Why don't others do it the way that you do?

_____

_____

What are the material payoffs of your solution?

_____

_____

_____

From the perspective of your clients or customers, what is superior about your approach?

_____

_____

How is doing things this way benefitting you and helping you stand apart?

_____

_____

What are the costs and compromises of your approach?

_____

_____

_____

What have you learned about your business by talking about your industry to strangers?

_____

_____

_____

How has this impacted the way that you make and implement decisions?

_____

_____

_____

What feedback have you received that has been vital to changing your approach?

_____

_____

_____

What feedback have you received that was safe to disregard?

_____

_____

_____

Mass production model
ex. Making coolers with
speakers in them in China
Advantage: scalable with PFC

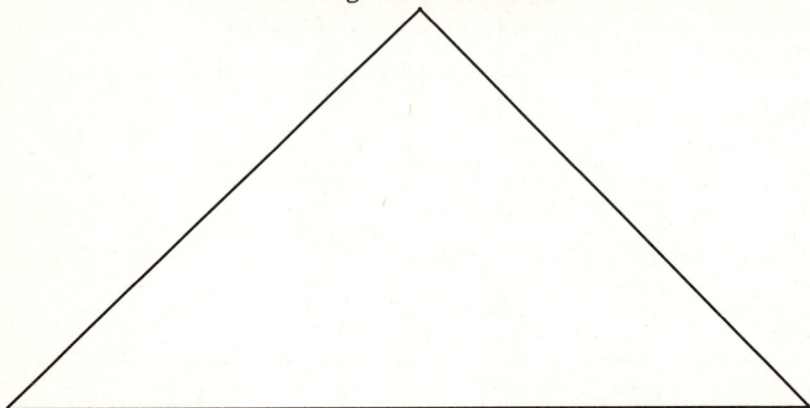

Automation model
ex. Setting up and owning
a business with outside
management
ex: Owning an Verizon store
Advantage: Passive income

**Service-oriented/Labor-
intensive model**
ex. Consulting, freelancing,
therapy, car repair
Advantage: Bigger profit margins

The above graphic shows a few different options for how a business can be structured. Regardless of your type of business, you can use this as a jumping-off point for thinking about the structure of your own business. Businesses have a tendency to embrace multiple structures as a measure to ensure cash flow, but doing so distracts from your fundamentals. So think carefully about which of these three structures best suits your business.

Draw the structure of your organization at present:

Now draw the structure of your organization next year:

GROWTH METRICS

*A*nother important thing to consider from the outset is growth. The following questions will help you think about how your business can expand in a coherent and sustainable way.

How can you test your idea's proof of concept in a small way?

_____

_____

How can you grow your idea by 5–25% every month for the next two years?

_____

_____

Do all aspects of your business successfully and effectively build on one another?

_____

_____

Where does your business function as a series of disparate ideas to increase cash flow rather than as a coherent whole?

_____

_____

ESTABLISHING YOUR GOALS

*I*n addition to meeting growth metrics, you probably have a lot of other goals in mind for your business. Use this exercise to home in on those goals and stay motivated to achieve them.

1. Write down a list of your top 25 business goals.

_____   _____

_____   _____

_____   _____

_____   _____

_____   _____

_____   _____

_____   _____

_____   _____

_____   _____

_____   _____

_____   _____

_____   _____

_____

2. Circle the 5 most important goals and cross off the other 20. Focus on the top 5.

3. Break each of these 5 goals down into steps.

Goal:

Steps:

Goal:

Steps:

Goal:

Steps:

Goal:

Steps:

Goal:

Steps:

4. Pin them to the wall next to your desk where you'll look at them every day.

5. Each week, revisit them and create another actionable step towards at least one of them.

FIGURING OUT YOUR MISSION, VISION, VALUES, AND BRAND

N ow that you've reflected on some of the fundamentals, let's get into the specifics of how you envision your business and your brand.

Mission

Who cares the most about what you're doing?

_____

_____

What do you fundamentally have to offer them that nobody else does?

_____

_____

Why do they care?

_____

_____

How are you able to solve their problems better than anyone else?

_____

_____

In what ways do you make their lives better? Brainstorm a list of 20 ways.

_____   _____

_____   _____

_____   _____

_____   _____

_____   _____

_____   _____

_____   _____

_____   _____

_____   _____

_____   _____

Look at your list. What are the three major themes that keep recurring?

_____

_____

_____

Now distill these themes and answers into the simplest sentence possible. This is your mission statement; it's how you describe the purpose of your business every day. A mission statement isn't usually very specific; rather, it prompts the listener to request more information. Some examples of mission statements would be "books to change your life and the world around you" and "innovative technology solutions for a better tomorrow." If Joe was writing a mission statement for a therapist, it would be "Magickal Counseling Practice strives to establish positive, trusting relationships that honor and respect clients' humanity while giving them tools to move forward successfully in life."

_____

_____

Once you've got your niche figured out, expand your one-sentence mission statement into a paragraph listing your business's unique strengths and benefits.

_____

_____

_____

_____

_____

_____

Vision

Brainstorm some keywords associated with your business and write them here in the form of a word cloud.

Now focus this brainstorm into a single narrative about what you want to accomplish that you tried to cram into your mission statement.

_____

_____

_____

In order to further home in on your vision statement and your understanding of your unique value proposition, answer the following questions:

What are the deadlines for each of your modest goals?

_____

_____

What are the deadlines for each of your ambitious goals?

_____

_____

_____

_____

_____

Imagine you have to give an accounting of your work—your best work—and you only have five minutes to do so. What would you say?

_____

_____

_____

_____

_____

_____

_____

_____

_____

_____

_____

_____

_____

_____

_____

_____

_____

_____

_____

_____

_____

_____

_____

_____

_____

_____

_____

_____

_____

_____

_____

Now write what you would say if you only had five seconds:

_____

_____

Next, write a one-sentence vision statement. This should communicate what you eventually want to accomplish that would make your business plans obsolete—a goal so large that you may *never* accomplish it completely. Some examples: "to radically reshape the publishing industry from the ground up"; "to create a world where mental health is prioritized and everyone is cared for"; "to become the premier purveyor of the best coffee with unyielding principles at scale"; or "to transition the world to electric cars through enviable design and culture."

_____

_____

Values

"Values" is another one of those terms that we see thrown around in a way that makes us think, "Wow, super important," and almost simultaneously, "What the fuck does that mean, though?" What's interesting about the word "value" is that it is a synonym of the word "worth." It means *what we hold in high regard.* What deserves our attention.

What is most important to you in life? How we describe and perceive ourselves is usually a reflection of our values. Our business decisions should come from what we hold most valuable.

If there is a disconnect between our values and our actions, this is a chance to pay attention to that experience and set ourselves back on course.

The big challenge for many people is defining what *our* values are, rather than the values that others have imposed upon us—whether those people were our parents or other caretakers when we were young, our friends, our peers, our partners, or society as a whole.

So let's figure out your bigger-picture values that drive all your life decisions, including in business.

Values Clarification

Many people don't have a language to articulate their values. Why does that matter in business? Because losing sight of your values is one of the biggest ways to fail as a business (eventually) and as an authentic human (almost immediately). Would Elizabeth Holmes and Theranos have caused the outrageous damage they caused if Ms. Holmes had worked in alignment with her values? So here's a huge list of potential values, plus space to write more of your own. Circle the ones that are important to you. Then use a different-colored pen or pencil to circle ones that aren't currently prominent in your life but that you *want* to be more important to you. This is all in service of not being the next Elizabeth Holmes. Or Sam Bankman-Fried, the FTX dickweed. Or Pharma Bro (sorry, too disgusted with him to look up his actual name, you know who I mean). Or whoever else has shocked and appalled you with their business behavior in recent memory.

Acceptance

Badassitude

Accountability

Accuracy

Achievement

Adaptability

Advocacy

Allyship

Ambition

Artistic expression

Artistic interactions

Assertive

Attentive

Balance

Beauty

Boldness

Bravery

Brilliance

Calm

Candor

Carefulness

Certainty

Challenge

Clean

Clear

Clever

Comfort

Commitment

Common sense

Communication

Community

Compassion for animals

Compassion for fellow humans

Competence

Concentration

Confidence

Connection

Consciousness

Consistency

Contentment

Contribution

Control

Convenience

Conviction

Cool

Cooperation

Courage

Courtesy

Creation

Creativity

Credibility

Curiosity

Decisiveness

Defeating fascism

Dependability

Design

Determination

Development

Devotion

Dignity

Discipline

Discovery

Dismantling oppressive systems

Dynamic

Effective

Efficient

Empathy

Empowerment

Endurance

Energy

Enjoyment

Enthusiasm

Social Justice

Ethical

Excellence

Experience

Exploration

Expressive

Fairness

Family	Health	Love
Fame	Honesty	Loyalty
Fearless	Honor	Magic
Feelings	Hope	Mastery
Feminism	Humility	Maturity
Intersectionality	Humor	Meaning
Ferocious	Hygge	Moderation
Fidelity	Imagination	Motivation
Focus	Independence	Nazi-Punching
Foresight	Individuality	Nesting
Fortitude	Influence	Neutrality
Freedom	Innovation	Openness
Friendship	Insight	Optimism
Fun	Inspiring	Organization
Generosity	Integrity	Originality
Genius	Intelligence	Passion
Giving	Intensity	Patience
Goodness	Intuition	Peace
Grace	Irreverent	Performance
Gratitude	Joy	Persistence
Greatness	Justice	Physicality
Growth	Kindness	Playfulness
Happiness	Knowledge	Poise
Hard work	Lawful	Potential
Tenacity	Leadership	Power
Hard-working	Learning	Practical
Harmony	Logic	Present

Productivity

Professionalism

Prosperity

Purpose

Queerness

Questioning authority

Realistic

Reason

Recognition

Reflective

Relaxation

Representation

Respect

Responsibility

Results-oriented

Righteousness

Rigor

Risk

Satisfaction

Security

Self-care

Self-compassion

Self-reliance

Selflessness

Sensitivity

Serenity

Service

Sexuality

Sharing

Silence

Simplicity

Sincerity

Skill

Solitude

Spiritual

Spontaneous

Stability

Status

Stewardship

Storytelling

Strength

Structure

Success

Support

Surprise

Tree-hugging

Teamwork

Sobriety

Thorough

Thoughtful

Timeliness

Tolerance

Toughness

Traditional

Transparency

Trust

Truth

Understanding

Uniqueness

Unity

Vigor

Vision

Vulnerability

Wealth

Welcoming

Winning

Wisdom

Wonder

Have values that aren't on this list? Write in your own.

Honoring Your Values

Now let's put those values to work. You've got your core values circled (kicking workbook ass!!!!), so now's the time to funnel those ideas into action for your business.

Use this worksheet to plan out how your business will embody the values you identified as the ones you would most like to live by. You can focus on changes you want to make around how you earn, spend, save, or feel about money, or anything else that's becoming clear to you as you do these exercises.

Value	Actions I need to take	Limits I need to set

Brand

How have your competitors managed their brands?

_____

_____

What makes your brand different?

_____

_____

Which brands are built around price or value?

_____

_____

Which brands are built on pretension or implicit reputation?

_____

_____

What is your brand based on?

_____

_____

_____

What do you want your brand to say about your work?

_____

_____

_____

Why?

_____

_____

_____

What are the feelings associated with your brand?

_____

_____

_____

How much sass does your brand have?[1]

_____

_____

_____

Are you spirited or bland?

_____

_____

_____

How does your company consistently uphold your brand's values?

_____

_____

_____

_____

_____

How does your website tell your brand's story?

_____

_____

_____

_____

How does your logo tell your brand's story?

_____

_____

_____

_____

_____

---

1 A reviewer called Joe's book, *A People's Guide to Publishing*, "a landmark treatise on sass" and said "that alone is reason enough to read it." No review will ever top that one.

WHAT'S HOLDING YOU BACK?

*A*ny personal baggage you're carrying around will hold you back in business. Some of the most common ways people undermine themselves in the professional world are through imposter syndrome, fear of failure, and self-sabotage.

Imposter Syndrome

Imposter syndrome was first operationalized by researcher Dr. Pauline Rose Clance, based on her work in clinical settings. She defines it as "a psychological phenomenon in which people are unable to internalize their accomplishments." Is imposter syndrome affecting you? Likely so if you are reading this section. It comes knocking for most of us at some point in our lives, so let's deal with it now so it doesn't come Godzilla-ing through your life when you least expect it.

Use the following questions to reflect on how you suffer from imposter syndrome.

1. How do you overprepare or procrastinate?

_____

_____

_____

2. When does success feel like a matter of effort instead of skill acquisition?

_____

_____

_____

3. Write a story about a time when you were the best at something and it created a cycle of feeling inadequate ever since.

_____

_____

_____

4. When do you exert enormous pressure on yourself? Is the need to be superhuman more about perfectionism than success? Does it feel fucked up if you aren't perfect?

_____

_____

_____

_____

_____

_____

_____

5. Do you overwork due to fear of failure? Do you need to be perfect or the best? Are you afraid of all performance-based tasks? Do you over prepare and suffer exhaustion?

_____

_____

_____

_____

_____

_____

6. Do you discount praise and deny your own competence? Do you attribute all your success to overpreparing? Do you find it difficult to accept positive feedback and praise? Do you feel discomfort with your own success? Do you argue with people who feel otherwise?

_____

_____

_____

_____

_____

_____

_____

_____

7. Do you feel fear and guilt about success? Does success make you feel anxiety that more will be expected of you?

_____

_____

_____

8. Do you suffer from self-sabotage as a result of your imposter syndrome? Does your imposter syndrome set you up for failure in preconscious ways?

_____

_____

_____

_____

9. Does your self-sabotage show up as disorganization, indecisiveness, perfectionism, burnout, constant anxiety, and procrastination?

_____

_____

_____

10. Do these maladaptive tendencies show up to customers and vendors?

_____

_____

Ok, reflection time. What did you connect with? What patterns did you notice? Don't worry, we don't expect you to look at all that and say, "Well, I'm fucked." It's just the first step, which is to become aware of our patterns. Now let's use the following questions to combat those patterns.

Write down every time that you've been successful in the past month.

_____

_____

_____

_____

Write down every time that you've been successful in the past year.

_____

_____

_____

_____

Which people in your life give balanced, accurate, and loving feedback?

_____

_____

_____

_____

Whose success do you admire? What can you learn from how they react to and embrace it? How do they continue to produce challenging and engaging work despite success and criticism in their past?

_____

_____

_____

_____

How do you want to handle success differently from how you handle it now?

_____

_____

_____

_____

How can you handle imperfection differently?

_____

_____

_____

_____

How do you handle not achieving what you want to achieve?

_____

_____

_____

_____

How do you learn and grow from those moments?

_____

_____

_____

_____

We Either Win or We Learn: Accepting Failure

Not to seem like one of those goofy mindset memes, but failures are events. Not people. If we want to be extra cute about it, we can look at the word as an acronym. Meaning F.A.I.L. stands for our "first attempt in learning." Cheesy but annoyingly true. I have learned far more from my failures than from my successes, though success feels much nicer in the moment. Some of my most effective business practices came to be because I did something unskillfull, unthoughtful, or just so fucking stupid I got my ass handed to me on a platter and I had to correct my bullshit. Here is a framework to help you see how anything that doesn't go as planned is still giving you gifts of experience:

Reflect on a time when your performance was not what you wanted it to be. When you perceived that you had failed.

_____

_____

_____

_____

Now write three things you learned as a result of this failure. What helpful (therefore, positive . . . sorry!) lessons did you learn about the situation, other people, yourself? If you have more than three, that's great, list them all. If you can't think of three, that's ok . . . list whatever you can.

_____

_____

_____

_____

_____

_____

_____

If you are sharing this process with a friend, therapist, or mentor, ask them if they noticed anything helpful you gained from the process.

_____

_____

_____

_____

_____

How do you want to handle failure differently?

_____

_____

_____

_____

_____

Self-Sabotage

Self-sabotage. One of the biggest hobgoblins we have to overcome. Self-sabotage refers to the ways that we either actively or passively prevent ourselves from achieving our goals. Who would act in ways that are counterproductive to their goals? Most people, honestly. If we have a history of failure—or of being told we are failures/stupid/lazy/not good enough/etc., especially as children—we internalize this as a rule about the world. And if we are hustling hard and moving towards success? Those tapes can start replaying in our heads. At a preconscious level, we start doing things to put ourselves back in line with the meta-message of failure that we've internalized: procrastination, lack of follow-through, reactionary behavior, etc.

We often don't recognize what we are doing as self-sabotage until our fuckery lands us in a dumpster fire of our own creation. But according to Katherine Hurst (writing for thelawofattraction.com), if we reverse engineer our patterns, we can learn to spot the signs. So let's start by building awareness of our own patterns. After each marker of self-sabotage, make some notes about whether and how you express this particular pattern in your life.

1. Obsessing Over the Negative

Yes, it's important to have a realistic picture of the world and your place in it. However, this means balancing the good and the bad.

If you find that you always look for a reason to view things as boring, dangerous, unachievable, or negative in any other way, then this is a serious warning sign that you need to work on overcoming self-sabotage.

When you focus exclusively on the negative, you attract more negativity into your life, and you restrict your own opportunities by finding excuses not to do things. Plus, if you're an extremely negative person, you reduce the number of people who want to be around you (effectively self-sabotaging relationships).

_____

_____

_____

_____

2. Immersion in Fear

Fear is linked to self-sabotage. If you've noticed that most things fill you with dread and terror, you might have hit upon what causes self-sabotaging behavior in your life. You might just feel fear in a specific area (e.g., related to romantic relationships), or it might be universal.

Either way, fear keeps you trapped and prevents you from fulfilling your full potential. While this is a sign of self-sabotage, it's also important to note that you might need additional help for an underlying anxiety disorder.

_____

_____

_____

_____

3. Underestimating Your Own Worth

If you tend to have low self-esteem, you likely have a particularly loud inner critic whose voice tells you that you can't do certain things. It might tell you that you're not attractive enough to date, or not smart enough to apply for a job. No matter what, if you tend to view yourself in an especially negative light, this is a clue that you may have self-sabotaging patterns.

Learning how to stop self-sabotaging in this case has a lot to do with adjusting your negative self-talk. In addition to doing work around your self-sabotaging behaviors, it's also worth practicing daily affirmations. These will rewrite some of the limiting beliefs that lead to you regularly sabotaging your own success.

_____

_____

_____

_____

4. Constant Comparisons

Another common indication of self-sabotage is a compulsion to compare yourself to others. Naturally, there are times when we all wish we had a quality or ability belonging to another person. However, if you're doing this with increasing frequency and you're using it as an excuse not to emerge from your comfort zone, you're engaging in self-destructive behavior.

For example, if you don't bother trying online dating because you think your friends on the website are more attractive, you're simply finding a way to avoid risk.

The truth is that there is enough success and happiness in the world for everyone. We all have something unique to give to the world. It's important to find the traits and skills you bring to the table that no one else does and to capitalize on those as much as possible.

_____

_____

_____

_____

5. Reversing Achievement

Perhaps the most obvious sign of self-sabotaging behavior is achieving something and then reversing this achievement.

In a relationship, this might take the form of getting to know someone you really like and then doing something to damage that connection (e.g., infidelity, avoidance, or changing behavior).

Meanwhile, at work, you might get a promotion and then end up failing to meet the major targets you've been set.

These types of experiences are all part of your self-sabotaging subconscious mind's attempts to push you back into a "safe," familiar place. They're also a way of proving to yourself that you were right to think you couldn't do certain things.

_____

_____

_____

_____

_____

6. Pushing People Away

Self-destructive attitudes towards relationships don't just appear in your dating life. If you tend to push people away in general, you're likely self-sabotaging. There are many different ways of pushing people away, ranging from being evasive in conversation to refusing to meet up or being outright rude or dismissive.

If you're a self-saboteur, you may often kick yourself for doing this once the damage to the relationship is already done, asking yourself why you've pushed yet another person away.

It will take conscious effort to learn new patterns.

_____

_____

_____

_____

7. Lacking Purpose

A final sign of self-sabotaging behavior is a sense that you lack purpose. You might feel listless day after day, never really knowing what you're "supposed" to be doing with your life.

Like the other self-sabotaging behaviors, this is often a way of staying safe and avoiding risky new experiences. After all, if you don't acknowledge and pursue a life purpose, you can't really fail or get hurt.

_____

_____

_____

_____

Now keeping those markers in mind, let's personalize what self-sabotage looks like for you and your business:

How would you define self-sabotage?

_____

_____

_____

What does the concept mean in regards to your circumstances?

_____

_____

How do you think self-sabotaging behaviors impact your well-being and the success of your business? For example, what are the short- and long-term consequences?

_____

_____

_____

_____

How do you sabotage things in your life?

_____

_____

Can you identify any particular patterns?

_____

_____

What replacement behaviors can you start using in response to these patterns? And we don't mean stuff like "stop thinking that way"— we're talking about very concrete strategies. Like, "When I notice my overwhelm and avoidance cycle, I am going to take a quick breathing break, then spend 15 minutes working on the problem I'm avoiding to remind myself what progress looks like. I don't have to solve it, I just have to work on it."

_____

_____

What can help you with the accountability part of this plan? Ensuring accountability is a proven way to make yourself more likely to stick to new habits. So, who can you tell about your new commitment to a sabotage-free life? You might discuss it with a friend, partner, family member, colleague, or combination of all of these. Try to check in with this person (or these people) regularly, discussing how your journey is progressing.

_____

_____

Part Two:

Strengthen What You Have

*T*he first part of this workbook focused on your vision for your business and the fundamentals of getting started. Now we're going to shift gears and think about how to improve your business and keep it running smoothly. Part Two will give you the tools to make your systems more efficient, keep your priorities aligned, and evaluate your progress.

BUILD IT

*A*s your business grows and you hire more people, your systems will become more complex. Rather than handling every task and decision yourself, you'll need to delegate. Complete this worksheet to figure out how to optimize your company's workflows.

Draw the path of decision making through every department at your company.

Think of 10 tasks that you perform weekly. For each, ask yourself, "When I do this, what is the usual outcome? What is the desired outcome?" Now draw a simplified and more streamlined version of your path of decision making that accomplishes the same thing more efficiently:

In the following chart, list all major tasks that must be performed on a weekly, monthly, quarterly, or annual basis.

For each one, list who is responsible for completing it and its priority level. List any dependent tasks relying upon that task, as well as who is responsible for those.

Next, for each task, list how much busier or larger you'd have to grow before it needs to be reassigned.

Major Task	Person Responsible	Priority Level	Dependent Tasks	When to Reassign

Which tasks performed at regular intervals could benefit from a checklist?

_____

_____

_____

What are the checklists and flow charts for every department?

When people arrive in the morning, is it clear who's responsible for what? Do your employees know when it's time to work down a checklist, or do all actions and decisions have to go through you?

_____

_____

_____

_____

_____

_____

_____

_____

_____

_____

Which tasks could be made less cumbersome and more efficient? In what ways could this improve workflow between departments?

_____

_____

_____

_____

_____

_____

_____

_____

Are there any tasks that you don't have the fundamental skills to be performing and that you should therefore assign to someone else? Which ones?

_____

_____

_____

_____

For each task, is it sufficiently clear—both in job descriptions and duties—who does what?

_____

_____

_____

_____

Are there tasks in your workflow that the wrong people are consistently doing or that cause people to step on each other's toes? Which ones?

_____

_____

_____

_____

If someone is unclear on whose domain a task falls into, is it clear who they should ask?

_____

_____

_____

_____

How clear is the sequence of priorities for each person in their workflow?

_____

_____

_____

_____

CONNECTING WITH YOUR AUDIENCE

No matter what kind of business you have, that business has a target audience, and you need to be able to find that audience and communicate with them. These questions will help you do just that.

Where do people already share a common interest in what you are doing?

_____

_____

_____

_____

_____

How do you maintain proximity and conversation with your fans?

_____

_____

_____

_____

What do your fans love?

_____

_____

_____

_____

What pisses off your fans?

_____

_____

_____

_____

What have your fans been seeking for years?

_____

_____

_____

_____

_____

How does your platform uniquely suit your fans?

_____

_____

_____

_____

_____

How can you employ Blue Ocean Strategy (selling where you don't encounter competitors) in reaching your fans?

_____

_____

_____

_____

_____

_____

HOW TO GET SCALE

*T*he adage about planning to fail and failing to plan may apply here: you need to think ahead to five years down the road in order to arrive there. This means you need to think some more about the growth of your business.

Which tasks will you never outgrow, even as the business grows?

_____

_____

_____

_____

_____

When will your growth require you to change your funding strategy?

_____

_____

_____

_____

Which aspects of your business should you focus on more as it grows?

_____

_____

_____

_____

How do you plan your growth as you succeed and double in scale? When will you need to grow facilities and staffing?

_____

_____

_____

_____

Would your current systems work at double your current size? Five times your current size?

_____

_____

_____

_____

Creating your own path from here to there is called "systems thinking." In what ways have you gone along with solutions that are offered or standard in your industry?

_____

_____

_____

_____

_____

In which cases are these solutions serving you? In which cases are they not serving you?

_____

_____

_____

_____

_____

The following graphic breaks down the considerations every time that you do something.

How to Make a Decision

What is my desired outcome?

What is the simplest solution to achieve it? Is there an easier way?

Does my idea work for everybody involved?

Y / N   STOP

Are the costs & consequences acceptable?

Y / N   STOP

What are the worst, best, and likely outcomes? Can I manage them all?

Y / N   STOP

Does this decision cause harm to anyone I care about and/or our relationship?

STOP   Y / N

Does this decision take too much time and energy
from the things I want and need to do?

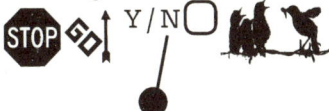

STOP   Y / N

Could this decision cost more money than I can afford? Is there a cheaper way?

STOP   Y / N

DO IT!

LEVERAGE

everage is what happens when we work together on a plan, rather than each person doing what they individually think is important. Think of how a mediocre bicyclist can go faster than an Olympic jogger with the help of a very simple machine—because all of the parts are working together. Another example: Microcosm built WorkingLit software in 2001 to manage our royalties, order fulfillment, billing, inventory, reprints, customer management, title management, and ONIX and EDI exports. A computer can do all of these things much more efficiently than any person. Then, by dividing people into departments, we ensure that they can focus on work and understand all of their pieces more thoroughly than they would if every person had to understand the entire picture. Look at leverage in two ways:

- The way that every hour worked and dollar spent serves your long-term goals and propels you towards them. As the manager or owner, your value is at least as great as anyone else's, and hopefully greater.
- Look at the big picture, how all of the parts work together towards the desired outcome. This way, we are greater than the sum of our parts.

Through utilizing these two aspects of leverage so effectively in tandem these past few years, we have grown faster than 99.99% of other publishers, while still being able to finance that growth through book sales. This section of the workbook will help you do the same.

In short, any money that you spend should be making you money. Preferably in at least equal doses. This money doesn't go in your pocket; it goes into growing your operations over time.

To improve leverage, you need to answer these questions: Which tasks are **urgent,** meaning there is a time crunch or you will lose your chance? And which tasks are **important**, meaning the stakes are high or there are potentially big rewards?

Write each major task in the appropriate column of the following worksheet.

Task	Urgent	Vital	Impor-tant	How does this move you towards your goals?

How often do you find that you are focused on tasks that are neither urgent nor important?

_____

_____

_____

_____

What is your system for making sure that the next task that you perform is always **urgent** or **important**?

_____

_____

_____

How can you better utilize your time to help plan for the future?

_____

_____

_____

How can you better utilize your staff towards targeted goals?

_____

_____

_____

_____

What is the next possible disaster that you can prevent?

_____

_____

_____

What is the next goal that you'd like to accomplish?

_____

_____

What task has the greatest leverage *right now*?

Do you frequently misjudge how long a particular task will take? Which task? Why do you feel that you have time blindness around this task?

Think of a time when you assigned a task to someone. What is the outcome of that task supposed to be? What is it actually producing?

ALIGN THE VALUE CHAIN

Remember our discussion of the value chain in Part One? Now we're going to dig deeper into what aligning your value chain looks like. As an example, let's review a published book from acquisition to reprint. The job of a publisher is to make the author's intellectual property more valuable—in all senses of the word—than it was previously. Here are the ways that our books create value for all parties:

- Our books are significantly different from those from other publishers. This helps retailers appeal to younger customers who are interested in subject matter that other publishers are not addressing in the same way.

- We repeatedly get feedback that Faith's first book, *Unfuck Your Brain*, feels more authentic to readers than other books on the same shelf.

- Microcosm and Faith have been working together for seven years and have sold five million books together. *Unfuck Your Brain* is now available in over 30 languages, and we just sold out of its 29th English printing. We adapted a middle reader version and published a Spanish edition. The audiobook outsold all of Stephen King's books in 2021, landing in the top 10 titles on all platforms. In 2022, it was the number three book in Italy.

- When we keep costs down and support the sales of a title, everyone benefits up and down the value chain. The printing cost of each copy dropped from $1.59 to $.62 by the fourth printing, as we were producing larger and larger print runs and selling them out before they reached the warehouse.

- The printer benefits from the reprints.

- 12,517 stores that order from Microcosm get the largest percentage of the cover price.

- The author gets significantly larger and larger royalty checks.

- The readers love the book and tell their friends.

- Microcosm can develop new projects with the increased cash flow.

- Joe has a reason to get out of bed every day. (Faith tries to avoid getting out of bed because she owes Joe an overdue manuscript, but whatever.)
- When revenues exceed expenses, Microcosm's staff receives profit sharing.

Here's another example of how we align the value chain at Microcosm:

- In 2018, Microcosm gave notice to our distributor that we were going to resume self-distributing. We had learned everything we could from them, had come to take the costs and consequences of our decisions much more seriously, and could achieve more by using the hours exhausted in maintaining that relationship to run our own sales and distribution service instead. We thought that if we worked really hard, we could maintain the same scale. Within three months, our sales increased by 59%. Within four years, we had quintupled. We had eliminated a major choke point in reaching our audience.
- We went from directly selling to 600 stores in 2014 to 12,000 stores in 2024. These stores are largely independents that buy and sell more than chain stores do and rarely return unsold copies.
- We gave our field salespeople 50% larger commissions to sell older titles that we have excess quantities of in the warehouse.
- Once Faith had sold over one million books, I called her to explain that the next stage in her career should involve getting agented and approaching a larger publisher that could penetrate markets more deeply and build her next steps. She said, "I don't want to. I'd rather work with you."
- She might have also made a good business decision. This year, Bookscan reported that the 29 largest independent publishers increased their market share by 12% in the past year, taking it from the Big Five and smaller independents. This is why consolidation of publishers has become a major focus of the past 10 years, but apparently it's lonely at the top.
- During the trial over the proposed merger of Simon & Schuster and Penguin Random House, it was revealed that both companies have had flat sales for the past decade and the only way that they have successfully increased sales is by

distributing independent publishers. So being an independent is really the "right size," because you have a lot more flexibility and much more growth potential.

• When paper shortages hit books in 2020, we had to schedule print runs earlier and costs increased by 30%, but our years-long relationship with our printer helped us avoid most major disruptions. When another printer approached us, our primary printer lowered prices, explaining that we required less service than most publishers so we were worth keeping.

Your Value Chain

Draw your value chain, explaining how each person that touches your product benefits from doing so. Is the chain out of alignment anywhere? If so, in what ways? How can you align it?

Who controls the power in your industry? How could you change or step around that?

_____

_____

_____

_____

_____

_____

_____

_____

_____

_____

_____

_____

_____

_____

_____

_____

_____

_____

_____

_____

Make a list of all major activities that you can't perform in-house but that your company relies upon in order to do business. Who controls each of these activities?

Activity	Who controls it?

Now, revisit this list and circle strategic control points (anywhere in your value chain where every industry participant is heavily reliant on a single product, solution, or service) in your industry.

How can you operate around these control points?

_____

_____

_____

_____

What are your suppliers' incentives to work with you?

_____

_____

_____

What are your customers' incentives to work with you?

_____

_____

_____

What are your employees' incentives to work with you?

_____

_____

_____

Are everyone's incentives aligned when the system is working? Why or why not?

_____

_____

_____

_____

How could changes in your supply chain have a major negative impact on your business?

_____

_____

_____

_____

_____

_____

What can you do now to plan for these possibilities?

_____

_____

_____

_____

_____

_____

_____

_____

NEVER DRIVE FASTER THAN THE CAR IN FRONT OF YOU

So many business owners are just so overjoyed at the freedom of not working for their former employer that they don't consider that they are acting within the context of their industry and competitors. So understand what's happening around you before you start making moves.

What is the immediate environment of your business?

_____

_____

_____

_____

_____

_____

_____

_____

Do you work in tandem with or in proximity to your competitors, or do you work in isolation?

_____

_____

_____

_____

_____

_____

_____

_____

Now reflect some more on your competitors by filling out this chart.

Who are your competitors?	What are they doing?	What are they *not* doing?	Why aren't they doing it?	What gaps are they leaving for you in your market?	Why aren't they going after these gaps?

How can you make your competitors obsolete by adjusting your to-market model?

_____

_____

_____

_____

How can you reach your future evangelists—people who will spread the word about your business in a year or two?

_____

_____

_____

_____

Do this step-by-step exercise on the next page:

1. For a future decision that you are going to make, list every available option.
2. For each option that you might take, draw a branch for that strategic move.
3. For each strategic move, draw the desired and probable outcomes.
4. List every potential move your supplier or competitors might make in response.
5. For each strategic move, assess the outcome of each competitor's move with probabilities and impacts. In which cases do the supplier/competitor's moves nullify your desired outcome? In which cases can you still reach your desired outcome?
6. Circle the best outcomes for you.

What will likely change in the next year? Five years? Ten years?

_____

_____

_____

_____

_____

_____

How do you predict that you can change within this landscape?

_____

_____

_____

_____

_____

What is the future skill set that you will need?

_____

_____

_____

_____

_____

How should you build relationships accordingly?

_____

_____

_____

_____

_____

Outcome bias is the assumption that because someone succeeded, they are good at their job. Or, if they failed, it means that they are bad at their job. Often the reality is far more contextual. In *How to Decide*, Annie Duke explains the value in looking at the possible outcomes of past decisions, even ones with positive outcomes, to better understand ways that things could have been different and how we can't always take credit, even for positive outcomes; some of them are simply incidental and outside of our control.

Do this step-by-step exercise in the space below:

1. For a past decision that you made, list every available option you had.
2. For each option that you might have taken, draw a branch for that strategic move.
3. For each strategic move, draw the desired and probable outcomes.
4. List every potential move your supplier or competitors might make in response.
5. For each strategic move, assess the outcome of each competitor's move with probabilities and impacts. In which cases do the supplier/competitor's moves nullify your desired outcome? In which cases can you still reach your desired outcome?
6. Circle the best outcomes for you.

What could have gone differently if you had handled these choices differently?

_____

_____

_____

_____

_____

_____

What was inevitable and outside of your locus of control?

_____

_____

_____

_____

_____

_____

ALWAYS NEGOTIATE

*T*he goal of negotiating is to create an agreement that will continue to work for both parties for as long as possible. If you twist the agreement too far in your favor, the other party will terminate it at their earliest possible opportunity. If the agreement doesn't actually work for you, you will be forced to decide whether to end it or attempt to maintain a pleasant attitude while suffering the consequences of bad choices that you made.

By staying honest and congruent with your reality, you can better explain how you arrived at these solutions and where you can be flexible both now and in the future. Perhaps even more important, if the situation worsens and the other party behaves badly, you'll have a solid track record and reputation for communicating positively, and this will be remembered and recognized over time.

What is a specific agreement that you would like to renegotiate?

_____

_____

What do you stand to gain from this agreement? How does it serve your goals?

_____

_____

_____

_____

What do you have to offer? Why is the other party making this agreement with you and what do *they* stand to gain from it?

_____

_____

What new terms would you like to propose for this agreement?

_____

_____

Say the other party responds with a counteroffer. What terms are you willing to settle for? What would make you decide to walk away?

_____

_____

_____

_____

When do you plan to attempt this renegotiation?

_____

More broadly, what are some areas where you might be able to negotiate to make agreements better serve both parties for a longer period of time?

_____

_____

_____

Think of a specific agreement. What are the various costs and benefits? How does it serve your goals?

_____

_____

How are your decisions influenced by others' behavior or "the only way to do things"?

_____

_____

_____

In many cases, discussing previous issues prior to line editing a contract makes the other party more receptive to change and gets you deeper insight. What are some ways that you can renegotiate contracts, based on this experience?

_____

_____

_____

_____

PERSPECTIVE

Perspective is a difficult lesson to learn, but it's an invaluable tool for getting a handle on whatever problems you and your business are facing. To gain perspective on a specific problem, answer the questions below. You can even turn this exercise into a daily practice.

What is your biggest problem *right now*?

_____

_____

_____

_____

Why is it a problem?

_____

_____

_____

_____

How big of a problem is it?

_____

_____

_____

_____

What are the worst things that might happen as a result? What are the most likely things that might happen as a result? What are the best things that might happen as a result?

_____

_____

_____

_____

How are you planning ahead?

_____

_____

_____

_____

How can you resolve this in the simplest manner?

_____

_____

_____

_____

Now let's go a little deeper. Thinking of the same problem you considered above, answer the following:

What are you focusing on? Your own sense of overwhelm? The behavior of an employee? Get specific.

_____

_____

_____

_____

_____

_____

_____

What are you noticing? Come up with as many possibilities as you can. Which explanation seems most likely? For example, if you are feeling overwhelmed with deliverables and afraid of failure, what might the mechanism behind that feeling be? Is it because you were often called a failure when you were growing up? What buttons are being pushed?

_____

_____

_____

_____

_____

_____

Now, don't overly attach to that hypothesis, but follow it with curiosity. Does it hold up when you bear witness to how you are interacting with the world? Does it follow when you observe your own thoughts and feelings?

_____

_____

_____

_____

_____

_____

Now let's get a little CBT-ish[2] with it. Is your reactivity based in reality? And even if it is, are you negotiating with yourself in a helpful way? Maybe you aren't meeting your projected goal for the quarter . . . is calling yourself a failure helpful? Not in the least. Instead, tell yourself, "I didn't do what I intended . . . so here is my chance to learn from this experience to either hit my targets in the future or change them to something more readily achievable."

_____

_____

_____

_____

_____

_____

Make your decisions based on this more balanced thinking. You don't have to throw everything into the chuck-it bucket because you're in a

2 CBT is short for cognitive behavioral therapy, a hugely popular evidence-based practice that focuses on how your thoughts and feelings influence your behavior. It helps you unpack your automatic thoughts, rules about the world, and core beliefs so you can reframe situations in order to respond more effectively.

bad spot at this particular moment. Is what you are doing still better than working for someone else? Even if you are delivering pizzas as a side hustle in the evenings to make payroll? Or is this not the thing and you need to reevaluate this business as a viable entity? We're not trying to convince you to stay on a sinking ship; we just hope you will make decisions from a place of recognizing as many of the moving parts as possible so you have fewer regrets later.

EVALUATION

y this point, you've done a lot of work to establish your goals and strengthen your systems. But how do you take stock of how things are going? In this section, we'll focus on evaluating different aspects of your business so you can know what's working and what's not.

Evaluating Success

What do you ultimately want to achieve?

_____

_____

_____

_____

What are the key performance indicators that let you know when things are working or not?

_____

_____

_____

_____

If you've launched, what is working?

_____

_____

_____

_____

What is not working as expected?

_____

_____

_____

_____

Why are those things not working?

_____

_____

_____

_____

What is it that brought you into business in the first place?

_____

_____

_____

_____

What motivates you on a daily basis?

_____

_____

_____

_____

Evaluating Growth

Are you growing 5–20% per year? ◯ *Yes* | ◯ *No*

Can systems grow and scale at your rate of expansion without breaking? ◯ *Yes* | ◯ *No*

At this rate of growth, will you burn yourself out? ◯ *Yes* | ◯ *No*

Do you want to grow to a certain size and then stop growing or sell the company to someone else?

_____

_____

_____

_____

Evaluating Data

Are you regularly reviewing your data? What does it show you?

_____

_____

_____

_____

_____

_____

_____

_____

_____

_____

_____

_____

_____

_____

_____

_____

_____

_____

_____

_____

_____

_____

_____

_____

_____

_____

To help evaluate your data, fill out the following chart:

Metric	Period of Time	Rate of Change	Inven-tory	Ex-penses	Bottom Line Expense	Payroll Costs	Sales

Looking at your chart, what patterns do you see?

_____

_____

_____

_____

_____

_____

_____

What expenses are growing faster than your sales?

_____

_____

_____

_____

_____

_____

_____

In what ways are you planning for the future? In what ways could you plan better?

_____

_____

_____

_____

_____

The more categories you create, the more transparency you have and the more you can drill down deep into your data. Which areas of your operation are working? Where do you need to spend less?

_____

_____

_____

What are the checks and controls that let you know that you are doing well?

_____

_____

_____

_____

What are signs that suggest caution?

_____

_____

_____

_____

_____

_____

How are you measuring up against short- and long-term goals?

_____

_____

_____

_____

What tasks are falling behind or to the wayside?

_____

_____

_____

_____

_____

What is no longer necessary?

_____

_____

_____

_____

Which tasks need to be delegated?

_____

_____

_____

_____

When should you hire another person? When do you _need_ to hire another person? And what should that person be doing?

_____

_____

_____

_____

How do you set larger strategic goals?

_____

_____

_____

_____

_____

_____

_____

Next, look at these patterns and create another chart that predicts the future.

Compare monthly changes and project outward by the same percentage.

Metric	Period of Time	Rate of Change	Inven-tory	Ex-penses	Bottom Line Expense	Payroll Costs	Sales

Then add up all of your expenses and compare to your future income estimates to project future cash flow.

When will you have big bills due?

_____

_____

When will you have money to pay them?

_____

_____

When will you run out of money?

_____

_____

When will you have excess funds?

_____

_____

When can you give out bonuses safely?

_____

_____

Do you need to adjust schedules as a result?

_____

_____

How do these systems put checks and balances on activities and decision making?

_____

_____

_____

_____

_____

_____

_____

_____

What are some ways that you can use this information to create new systems?

_____

_____

_____

_____

_____

_____

_____

What could you accomplish through borrowing money? Would the cost of doing so outweigh the benefits?

_____

_____

_____

_____

What are other metrics, data sets, and information that would be useful to know at all times or at least keep track of?

_____

_____

_____

_____

_____

Evaluating Ideas

Are you open to suggestions and experimentation? Would you like to be more open to these things?

_____

_____

_____

Think of a specific change that you're considering and answer the following questions:

How do you think your customers would react?

_____

_____

_____

Who can you contact that you trust and can solicit feedback from?

_____

_____

_____

_____

How have you thoroughly evaluated all aspects of your idea to know that it's sound before proceeding?

_____

_____

_____

_____

What is a more ambitious goal that you can set?

_____

_____

_____

_____

How could simply aiming higher improve all of your decision making?

_____

_____

_____

_____

To determine if an idea is a good one, use the return-on-investment calculation: net income / (property + (assets - liabilities)).

Net income is income minus cost of sales, operational expenses, depreciation, interest, amortization, and taxes.

Property is the material purchase, like real estate, intellectual property, or inventory.

Assets are items that you can sell for cash value, like equipment.

Liabilities are the debts that you owe as a result of these activities—your bills.

This shows you what the best uses of your effort are, based on your costs and outcomes. Compare a few different options.

_____ / (_____ + (_____ - _____))
$\quad$ *net income* $\qquad$ */ (property* $\qquad$ + $\qquad$ *(assets - liabilities)).*

_____ / (_____ + (_____ - _____))
$\quad$ *net income* $\qquad$ */ (property* $\qquad$ + $\qquad$ *(assets - liabilities)).*

_____ / (_____ + (_____ - _____))
$\quad$ *net income* $\qquad$ */ (property* $\qquad$ + $\qquad$ *(assets - liabilities)).*

_____ / (_____ + (_____ - _____))
$\quad$ *net income* $\qquad$ */ (property* $\qquad$ + $\qquad$ *(assets - liabilities)).*

_____ / (_____ + (_____ - _____))
$\quad$ *net income* $\qquad$ */ (property* $\qquad$ + $\qquad$ *(assets - liabilities)).*

KNOW WHEN TO QUIT

*T*here's a point in every businessperson's life when they are simply burnt out over a period of years, or the industry has changed so much that the things that attracted them to it are no longer the same. It's important to know when to quit; otherwise, you'll simply be miserable, or—worse—your business will run you rather than the other way around. Drawing boundaries around any issues is the best way to maintain agency in your life, so use the questions below to figure out where those boundaries are when it comes to your business.

What changes in your industry would make your business obsolete?

_____

_____

_____

_____

Are expenses suddenly outweighing revenues? Why?

_____

_____

_____

_____

Are there ways that you can pivot to offset these changes and become relevant again? If so, list them here.

_____

_____

_____

_____

Are you combating burnout on a personal level? Is it a good time to hand over the reins to someone else, temporarily or permanently?

_____

_____

_____

Part Three:

Build Your
Skills and Team

In this final part of the workbook, we'll zero in on some specific skill sets to take your business to the next level. These include management, sales, customer service, and budgeting. The manager's most important job is keeping on top of these things.

As your business grows, you'll need to hire more people. This means you'll need to build your skills in managing others so that your business can reach its full potential. And that's not an easy task. Management is half morale and half spreadsheets, and it's a balancing act: it's important to give everyone room to do their job while still being aware enough to catch their mistakes—to say your piece and listen while standing your ground. And it all goes back to having fun. The exercises in this section focus on some of the key challenges of managing a team.

We aren't going to address layoffs or firing here, as managers tend to have a very cultural, fixed mindset about these things, depending on where they come from. In general, as long as your staff is productive, that's great. If there's nothing for them to do, layoffs may make sense. But in most cases, an employee can be moved into a higher-leverage job instead.

Leveraging Your Staff

The manager's job is to always be looking to replace yourself in the job that you are currently doing. Use the following questions to reflect on how you can do this.

In which departments is your capacity strained so much that it's making it difficult for you to focus?

_____

_____

_____

_____

What tasks can other people do better than you can?

_____

_____

_____

_____

Where will supplementing your own strengths create more value and build departments that are more robust?

_____

_____

_____

_____

_____

How can you get out of the way so that smart people can make smart decisions and be helpful foils for refining your good ideas into great ideas?

_____

_____

_____

_____

Team Culture

How do you think about the culture of your team? What words apply to certain team members? On the next page, circle the ones that apply and write in your own.

Advocate	Healer	Sage
Alchemist	Helper	Scientist
Amateur	Guide	Seeker
Ambassador	Go-Between	Seer
Analyst	Individualist	Servant
Anarchist	Innovator	Skeptic
Apprentice	Instructor	Sleuth
Arbitrator	Leader	Storyteller
Architect	Liberator	Student
Avenger	Mediator	Teacher
Builder	Mentior	Therapist
Caregiver	Messenger	Trickster
Challenger	Networker	Visionary
Champion	Philosopher	Wanderer
Communicator	Performer	Warrior
Companion	Observer	Wounded Healer
Creator	Protector	_____
Craftsperson	Rebel	_____
Defender	Redeemer	_____
Diplomat	Reformer	_____
Disciple	Revolutionary ———	_____
Engineer	Saboteur	_____

Taken together, what kind of culture do these roles create within your team?

_____

_____

_____

_____

_____

_____

_____

_____

_____

What steps do you take to maintain morale and curb negativity?

_____

_____

_____

_____

What is your mechanism for listening to people's concerns?

_____

_____

_____

_____

_____

How do you make sure your staff feels comfortable telling you what's really going on?

_____

_____

_____

_____

How do you show people that you care?

_____

_____

_____

_____

What are your staff's most important considerations in deciding whether to keep working for you? What are the benefits of the job as far as they are concerned?

_____

_____

_____

_____

_____

Where are team behaviors not matching company values?

_____

_____

_____

Do you maintain retention through rewarding staff with bonuses, or do you view your team as a commodity? Why?

_____

_____

_____

_____

How do you distinguish between what is frustrating people in the moment and what is a longstanding grievance?

_____

_____

_____

_____

How do you address longstanding frustrations and grievances so they do not fester and can be laid to rest?

_____

_____

_____

_____

Challenges and Feedback

In *Unfuck Your Business*, we suggest holding 10-minute weekly check-ins with each of your reports. What are the recurring themes of what you learn from these check-ins?

_____

_____

_____

_____

_____

_____

_____

When you offer performance feedback, what are the recurring key takeaways? What surprises your staff about your assessments?

_____

_____

_____

_____

What tasks and hurdles are continuing to cause the most difficulty for your staff?

_____

_____

_____

_____

How can you better set the tone to prepare them for these challenges and make their lives easier?

_____

_____

_____

_____

_____

How can your system grow, change, evolve, or benefit from the observations of your staff?

_____

_____

_____

_____

How important is it to your business (not to you) how tasks are performed by your staff? Is there an actual problem with the way things are done, or do you need to work on letting go of some control?

_____

_____

_____

_____

_____

_____

_____

Management Structure

Next we are going to determine whether your business favors a flat or hierarchical structure and decide which one would better support success.

For the following statements, circle true or false:

Most of my employees do not require much direct oversight to produce good results. ○ *True* | ○ *False*

Our company has a series of systems where much individual reflection and thinking is necessary before getting down to business. ○ *True* | ○ *False*

At my company, I can trust everyone to understand the individual metrics of their job duties and what makes them successful. ○ *True* | ○ *False*

Most employees at my company have a high level of autonomy. ○ *True* | ○ *False*

At my company, there is a strong need for mutual understanding among employees. ○ *True* | ○ *False*

If I didn't come to work for a week, outputs would proceed largely unaffected. ○ *True* | ○ *False*

At my company, the goals of most tasks are far more subjective than objective. ○ *True* | ○ *False*

Most workers are accountable to their tasks and goals rather than fear of termination. ○ *True* | ○ *False*

Your total number of "true" responses:

What Your Score Means:

0–3: Your business has a hierarchical management structure. There is a high level of rigidity and very little room for individual decision making. Employees are replaceable and cheap to train, and they conform to an existing role without much thought. Think about how this suits your self-image and how it will suit your business in several years. Could your business benefit from the ideas and opinions of your staff?

4: Your business is a hybrid of both hierarchical management and flat management, combining features of both models. What are some areas where you could benefit from additional employee input and ideas?

5–8: Your business likely has a flat management structure, meaning there is a relatively low level of supervision, a relatively high level of accountability for each team member, and a tremendous need for mutual understanding. This structure is less rigid than a hierarchical one. It can feel uncomfortable to realize this about your business, especially in the US, where most businesses lean towards a hierarchical structure.

Reflect briefly on why you chose your current management structure.

_____

_____

_____

_____

Is your current structure still working for your business? Or does it need to change?

_____

_____

_____

_____

Looking more closely at your staff, answer the following questions:

In what ways are your employees your competitive advantage?

_____

_____

_____

_____

Do you have any high performers who are endlessly sowing discontent or negativity? If so, how can you address this?

_____

_____

_____

_____

How is news distributed to your staff? Does this create the desired outcome?

_____

_____

_____

_____

_____

_____

What factors contribute to your ability to ask an honest question and receive an honest answer from your staff?

_____

_____

_____

_____

_____

_____

How do you acknowledge and respect the power differential between you and your staff?

_____

_____

_____

_____

_____

_____

_____

SALES

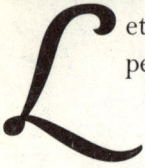

Let's take a look at your sales funnel, a way to introduce new people to what you are doing.

PEOPLE LEARNING ABOUT YOU

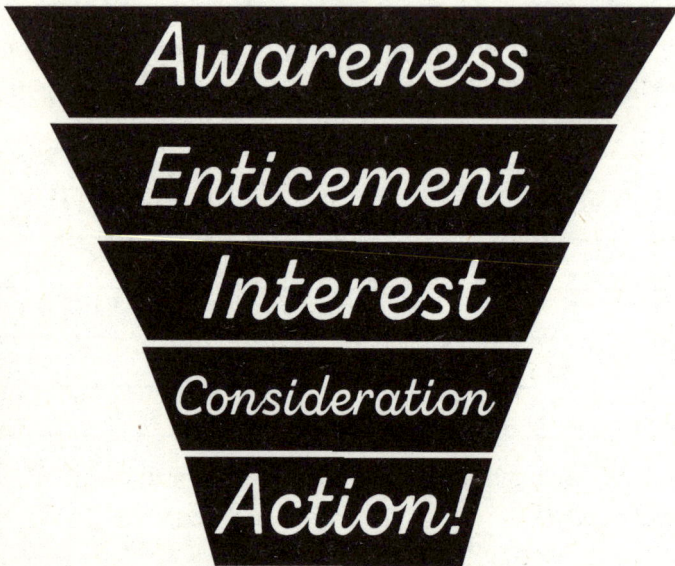

⬇

Awareness

Enticement

Interest

Consideration

Action!

- **Awareness:** How do you show your work to new audiences?
- **Enticement:** What is their attraction to purchase?
- **Interest:** What do people who immediately take you up on this offer have in common?
- **Consideration:** What do people who linger but do not buy have in common? Do they need more information? Do they need a discount? Do they not understand the payoff?
- **Action:** What do people have in common who choose to work with you after receiving all of the information? What is motivating them? How can you focus more effort around them?

Now draw your own funnel. What is happening materially at each stage in your business?

What is the best way to phrase your solution to your problem?

_____

_____

_____

_____

_____

_____

_____

What questions can you ask to bridge the gap between what you do and your customers' misconceptions about it?

_____

_____

_____

_____

_____

_____

How have people expressed interest in your business in ways other than an immediate purchase?

_____

_____

_____

_____

_____

What do you learn from rejections?

_____

_____

_____

_____

_____

How can you better explain your offering to weed out the wrong people and entice the right people?

_____

_____

_____

_____

_____

SERVICE

*T*here are two things that every customer will remember about your organization: the best deal you ever gave them and the biggest mistake you ever made, as well as how you resolved it. Understanding this is very helpful in crafting your service strategy.

What is a specific customer-service mistake your business has made recently and then repaired?

_____

_____

_____

How did you repair it?

_____

_____

_____

What is a customer-service mistake your business has made recently that has *not yet* been repaired?

_____

_____

_____

How much of a relationship do you have with the customer? How much of a relationship do you want?

_____

_____

_____

Generally, you should aim to make 80% of customers happy, because the other 20% will never be happy. Which category does this customer fall into? Do you think it's possible to make them happy?

_____

_____

_____

Based on your answers to the above questions, would it make sense to try to repair this situation? If so, what can you offer the customer that would fix the problem and restore their favorable view of your business?

_____

_____

_____

Now use the questions below to reflect on your customer-service systems:

What are your established systems and service-solution parameters for your staff to implement so that there is never a question about how to handle a standard situation?

_____

_____

_____

Who handles these problems for your company?

_____

_____

_____

Who will answer the phone and respond to messages from customers or clients?

_____

_____

_____

What promises can you make to customers or clients that you can keep?

_____

_____

_____

What is your system for hearing and addressing new problems?

_____

_____

When numerous customers have the same problem, how can you address the issue at its root?

_____

_____

_____

How can you make 80% of customers happy, even if you lose money on a few sales, so they come back next time?

_____

_____

_____

How can you identify the other 20% of customers that will never be happy so you don't put your effort into them?

_____

_____

_____

How can you identify problems faster, before someone else says there is a problem?

_____

_____

_____

MONEY AND INVESTMENT

*W*e can't talk about business without talking about money. From reflecting on your financial problems and feelings to creating your monthly budget to prioritizing expenses, this section will walk you through the basics.

Financial Snapshot

What are your biggest problems with money?

_____

_____

_____

Can you borrow money adequate to your needs? If not, what can you do about this?

_____

_____

_____

Have there been times when inadequate cash flow has been an asset because it's forced your business to innovate? If so, how can you implement these lessons into the daily structure of your business?

_____

_____

_____

Are there any ways in which having access to too much money has created more problems for your business? How so?

_____

_____

_____

What is your business's ideal relationship to money in the long run?

_____

_____

_____

Unpacking My Money Rules and Feelings

So much of this workbook centers around how you relate to money. Which may feel gross. The fact that money feels like such an uncomfortable, squicky topic is exactly why it is so important to look at it more closely.

What are the reasons for the squicky discomfort? None of us invented capitalism, but here we are having to live with it. And doubly so if we are small-business owners. So let's look at some of the underlying thoughts and feelings that might cause us to get in our own way.

Positives:

Confidence: I feel most confident about money when . . .

_____

_____

_____

Excitement: I feel most excited about money when . . .

_____

_____

_____

Security: I feel most secure about money when . . .

_____

_____

_____

Relaxation: I feel most relaxed about money when . . .

_____

_____

_____

Pride: I feel most proud about money when . . .

_____

_____

_____

Struggles:

Insecurity: I feel insecure about money when . . .

_____

_____

_____

Stress: I feel stressed about money when . . .

_____

_____

_____

Anxiety: I feel anxious about money when . . .

_____

_____

_____

Fear: I feel fearful about money when . . .

_____

_____

_____

Intimidation: I feel intimidated about money when . . .

_____

_____

_____

Embarrassment: I feel embarrassed about money when . . .

_____

_____

_____

Hopelessness: I feel hopeless about money when . . .

_____

_____

_____

Confusion: I feel confused about money when . . .

_____

_____

_____

Nervousness: I feel nervous about money when . . .

_____

_____

_____

Guilt: I feel guilty about money when . . .

_____

_____

_____

Sadness: I feel sad about money when . . .

_____

_____

_____

Your Monthly Budget and Schedule

Let's take a look at your monthly budget.

Complete the following chart for all your monthly expenses:

Expense Category	$ Amount	How Its Effectiveness Is Measured

What did you learn through this process?

_____

_____

_____

_____

_____

_____

Which operations are not on schedule? Why not? Is this temporary or a new normal?

_____

_____

_____

_____

_____

What is the plan and timeline to get them back on schedule?

_____

_____

_____

_____

_____

How do you know when to add capacity in a department?

_____

_____

_____

_____

_____

Evaluating Expenses

What is your next major expense? Does it benefit you by . . .

○ Providing you with a good or service that you need (like raw materials or staffing)?

○ Directing you towards specific, identified goals?

○ Offering incentives like credit card cash back rewards or travel benefits (e.g., free hotels or flights)?

○ Increasing sales?

○ Decreasing future expenses?

○ Expanding your market share?

If the expense doesn't benefit you in any of these ways, what is your plan to address this? How can you eliminate this expense?

_____

_____

_____

_____

_____

_____

_____

_____

Prioritizing Expenditures

Now that you have a sense of how to evaluate expenses to determine whether they're serving your business, let's work on prioritizing those expenses that are beneficial. Remember to reflect on your business's values as you complete this exercise, because we did that part first for a reason, right?

First, list the top five priorities for your business at this moment.

_____

_____

_____

_____

_____

Now that you have your priorities laid out clearly in front of you, answer these questions:

If your business had an extra $5,000 right now, where would it go?

_____

_____

_____

_____

_____

What category or categories does that expenditure fall under? Break it down. For instance a massage might fall under the categories of "employee care" "advertisement" and "new product development."

_____

_____

_____

_____

_____

Did the categories align with ones you consider higher priority?

_____

_____

_____

_____

_____

If not, was it because of the unique circumstances you are currently experiencing?

_____

_____

_____

_____

_____

_____

How were your priorities different from what you originally thought?

_____

_____

_____

_____

_____

_____

_____

_____

_____

_____

_____

Now what if it's $20,000?

_____

_____

_____

_____

_____

_____

_____

_____

_____

_____

_____

_____

_____

What about $100,000?

_____

_____

_____

_____

_____

_____

_____

_____

_____

_____

_____

_____

Make a Dream Expenditures List

Now you've done all this work unpacking the stuff that is most important for you to spend money on. Good for you. The next two exercises aren't about what is possible in the present—instead, they're about paying attention to what's important as you move into the future.

List out your big-ticket wish list items. These are things that aren't recurring monthly expenses but require a hefty payout upfront. You define hefty: that could mean $100 or $100,000. Your list might include things like starting a college tuition reimbursement for employees, purchasing a new warehouse, installing an organic garden on the top of your current warehouse, creating an on-site daycare for the children of your staff, or anything else you would like to do if money wasn't a consideration. Put a star or number next to your highest priorities:

PRIORITY	DREAM EXPENDITURES

Now list out the regular monthly expenditures you'd have room for in a dream budget. Things like the expenses associated with your new warehouse or your new warehouse roof garden. Also include items that don't have a hefty up-front cost but are an ongoing expense you don't currently have room for. Like the salary of a personal assistant who handles enough of your day-to-day matters that you have more freedom for new product development. Or a well-stocked snack fridge in the break room. A productivity coach who works with your team. Whatever. Put a star or number by your highest priorities:

PRIORITY	DREAM EXPENDITURES

Evaluating Your Funding Sources

How will you fund operations for the next year? Does it make more sense to fund with cash, to take out a loan, to create a public option, to borrow from people that you know, or something else?

_____

_____

_____

_____

When will this change? Why?

_____

_____

_____

_____

_____

_____

_____

_____

EXTERNAL ENTITIES

*A*s a business owner, you won't just have to interact with employees, customers, and clients—you'll also have to deal with various regulating agencies, as well as vendors. Use these questions to reflect on how you engage with these entities.

What taxes is your business responsible for?

_____

_____

_____

_____

_____

_____

_____

What regulating agencies apply to your business?

_____

_____

_____

What vendors will you need to depend on for your business?

_____

_____

_____

_____

_____

_____

_____

_____

Are there any of these tasks handled by a third party that make sense to handle yourself?

_____

_____

_____

_____

_____

_____

_____

_____

Are there any tasks handled in-house that make sense to be handled by a third party?

_____

_____

_____

_____

_____

_____

_____

_____

_____

_____

_____

_____

MAKING ROOM FOR CHANGE

One of the biggest sticking points for business owners is our struggle to recognize that we need to change. How many huge companies have you seen collapse because they didn't attend to how culture was moving? If you are an old person like we are, you can remember which companies thought the internet was a fad that they did not need to get on board with, right? Strategizing around these cultural shifts is difficult because humans hate change, no matter how inevitable it is. Here are some self-coaching strategies to get you in the right mindset for making change, borrowed from neuro-linguistic programming, which is a set of techniques designed to help us better understand our own minds. Use the following prompts to reflect on a specific change that you're considering.

Possible change:

_____

1. **Ask the questions that make you examine the status quo.** What underlies the desire to change? What is within your ability to change? What are your reasons for change? What makes the change needful? What is your commitment to change?

_____
_____
_____
_____
_____
_____
_____
_____
_____
_____

2. I'm so sorry, but you really got to do the pros and cons list. What is the good stuff about the status quo and what is the good stuff about changing from the status quo? What might be the problems with keeping within the status quo? What might be the problems associated with change?

_____

_____

_____

_____

_____

_____

_____

_____

_____

_____

3. Here is your space to expand on any of what you already wrote. In what ways would this be a good thing? In what ways may it not be? How do you see the process unfolding?

_____

_____

_____

_____

_____

_____

_____

_____

_____

_____

4. **Now map out some examples from above.** What other life experiences have you had that may relate to the change you are taking under consideration? What examples have you seen others go through?

_____

_____

_____

_____

_____

_____

_____

_____

_____

5. **Review the past for guidance.** You're needing to change for some reason, right? What made the status quo the best decision for you in the past, and what is different in the present?

_____

_____

_____

_____

_____

_____

_____

_____

_____

_____

6. Now futurecast. What's the most likely thing to happen if you don't make any changes? What about if you do?

_____

_____

_____

_____

_____

_____

_____

_____

_____

_____

_____

7. Now consider the possible extremes. What are the best-case scenarios? What is the worst? Which options best match what you want your future to look like?

_____

_____

_____

_____

_____

_____

_____

_____

_____

_____

_____

8. **Now scale your change.** I'm so sorry, but therapists love this ish, bear with me. On a scale of 0–10, with 0 meaning "not at all important" and 10 meaning "tsunami level of importance," how does this change feel right now? For what reasons is that number not lower? For what reasons is that number not higher? What would help you increase your level of change importance? What might happen if you did move up a number or so? What happens when you use these questions to quantify the other factors associated with change (e.g., need, desire, ability, and commitment)?

_____

_____

_____

_____

_____

_____

_____

_____

_____

_____

9. **Now review your values and your goals that are associated with those values.** How are these changes in alignment with your goals and values? How may they be at odds? Does this influence your process in any direction?

_____

_____

_____

_____

_____

_____

_____

_____

_____

_____

_____

10. Now review all of the above. Because adult decision making is
difficult, right? But seriously, look at all of the important data
points regarding changing versus staying the same. What do
you notice? Does your decision seem clearer at this point? Is
there any other information you need?

_____

_____

_____

_____

_____

_____

_____

_____

_____

_____

ANTICIPATING CHANGES

*A*s a business owner, you can never lose sight of the fact that the world around you is constantly evolving. So now that you've done the work of reflecting on a specific change you might like to make, let's zoom out and think about the society-wide trends and developments that could affect your business.

Technology

In what ways does technology affect your business?

_____

_____

_____

_____

_____

_____

What are the emergent technologies that could disrupt your business?

_____

_____

_____

_____

_____

_____

How are you responding to these changes now and in the future?

_____

_____

_____

_____

_____

_____

Globalization

Which aspects of your business are reliant upon global factors?

_____

_____

_____

_____

_____

Which raw materials can you not economically source locally?

_____

_____

_____

_____

What choke points does globalization create in your industry?

_____

_____

_____

How will globalization affect what you do in the next year? Five years? Ten Years?

_____

_____

_____

_____

_____

_____

THE LAST MILE

*L*ast mile problems are complications that arise in the final steps before a product or service reaches the customer. These problems are unique and specific to your exact business. Some examples: You send a shipment to a buyer, but then it sits in a warehouse in their town for weeks because there aren't enough delivery drivers. Or you have plenty of customers coming to your restaurant, but there's such a long line that m any of them give up and leave before being seated. The last mile is half of your cost, so take this opportunity to reflect on how this looks for your business.

What is the hardest aspect of reaching your customer where they are?

_____

_____

_____

_____

_____

How can you simplify this chain?

_____

_____

_____

_____

_____

How can you turn this challenge into a creative solution or advantage?

_____

_____

_____

_____

_____

CONCLUSION

So now that you've reached the end of this workbook, what's next? For one thing, we hope that as your business continues to grow and change, you'll return to some of the exercises to reflect on these changes and keep yourself and your business on track. And as you move forward, remember that the most important thing, as in any part of life, is to be open to continuing to learn every day. While I happened to land upon many of the critical principles of business by chance at a young age, I have had to learn new things every day since. In a consulting meeting with another publisher, the owner told me that she chose me because it was obvious that I learned new things every day. I had never thought of myself this way before, but it's absolutely true. It's what made me so good at my job, though again, I didn't even realize this until someone else pointed it out to me.

Learning new things every day is important for a number of reasons:

- It gives you a competitive edge.
- You won't approach a problem the same way as your competitors.
- You have a negotiating advantage because your methods will be unexpected.
- You will have clever and creative solutions to problems, adapted from other industries.

When planning a conference, I discovered that we were paying $40 per person for a breakfast of bananas, muffins, and juice. Most participants were oversleeping and not eating anyway, but our organization was paying thousands of dollars per meal for food that was wasted. The problem is that the food was contractually tied to the venue. I suggested moving the conference outside of a hotel with catering. One board member quipped that when they had planned a recent wedding, even tacos had cost $20 per person; food is just expensive. I pointed out that even if we spent $20 per person on tacos for every meal for every attendee and I ate the leftovers, we'd save $80,000 per year without cutting any services. We just needed to restructure how we envisioned the conference. We could pocket the upcharges instead of the hotel.

Similarly, your job is to think critically and outside the box. Then ask yourself, Do we want protein in our guests or sugar? Which one causes their brains to be more engaged for conference discussion?

Remember the four variables of supply, demand, scale, and access? You can approach those variables, make changes to how you engage them, or solve short-term gaps in one or all of them much more easily with creative and critical thinking adapted from other industries. Put simply by longtime Microcosm touring chef and cookbook author Joshua Ploeg, in his worst approximation of Donald Rumsfeld, "We go into the kitchen with the ingredients that we have, not the ingredients that we want."

Similarly, always remember the six key ingredients to success:

• Learning new things every day
• Eternally being an optimist
• Disregarding all bad news
• Doing what everyone tells you is impossible
• Keeping a sense of humor
• Recognizing good ideas before they are obvious in hindsight

Remember to always resist becoming set in your ways. Things change, situations evolve, and cultural dynamics undergo major shifts. Be willing to try new things and even old things that didn't work before. That is, as long as they serve your broadest strategic goals. And always ask this question: Is there room to grow your passion bigger?

RECOMMENDED READING

Blue Ocean Strategy: How to Create Uncontested Market Space and Make the Competition Irrelevant by W. Chan Kim and Renée Mauborgne

The Carrot and the Stick: Leveraging Strategic Control for Growth by William Putsis

The Gift of Fear: And Other Survival Signals That Protect Us from Violence by Gavin De Becker

Growing a Business by Paul Hawken

Dare to Lead: Brave Work. Tough Conversations. Whole Hearts. by Brené Brown

Decoded by Jay-Z

High-Output Management by Andrew S. Grove

The Listening Path: The Creative Art of Attention by Julia Cameron

Never Split the Difference: Negotiating as if Your Life Depended on It by Chris Voss and Tahl Raz

People Skills: How to Assert Yourself, Listen to Others, and Resolve Conflicts by Robert Bolton

A People's Guide to Publishing: Build a Successful, Sustainable, Meaningful Book Business by Joe Biel

Unfuck Your Worth: Overcome Your Money Emotions, Value Your Own Labor, and Manage Financial Freak-Outs in a Capitalist Hellscape by Dr. Faith G. Harper

Unfuck Your Boundaries: Build Better Relationships through Consent, Communication, and Expressing Your Needs by Dr. Faith G. Harper

What Every Body Is Saying: An Ex-FBI Agent's Guide to Speed-Reading People by Joe Navarro